f e a r l e s s l y

fragile

to everyone who ever made me feel like i was
enough

they said, you'll be someone else and just the same. they were right.

a written polaroid about being twenty-one

…

headfirst, fearless

…

they said, you'll be someone else and just the same. they were right.

a written polaroid about being twenty-one

content warnings for this one:

body shaming
fatphobia
eating disorders
familial and emotional abuse
sexual abuse
illegal prostitution
heartbreak
self-harming behaviors
self-loathing
loss and death

thank you for reading, feeling and healing with me <3

they said, you'll be someone else and just the same. they were right.

a written polaroid about being twenty-one

© 2024 Madison Diana Foit
Herstellung und Verlag:
BoD – Books on Demand, Norderstedt
ISBN: 9783757808709

they said, you'll be someone else and just the same. they were right.

a written polaroid about being twenty-one

let the woman pass
the father said
holding his son's hand
i'm wearing my best friend's dress
which reminds me of my mom's
in 2014

i pass by and realize
they were talking about
me

and i'm twenty-one

and no longer young and helpless

they said, you'll be someone else and just the same. they were right.

a written polaroid about being twenty-one

loving
not just the music but
the artist themselves

is like

loving someone for
who they are

instead of just crushing

on a favorite part of

them

-thank you, taylor

they said, you'll be someone else and just the same. they were right.

a written polaroid about being twenty-one

since i already got the
first thing
i cannot wait for
the second

one

-thank you again, taylor

they said, you'll be someone else and just the same. they were right.

a written polaroid about being twenty-one

singing on the balcony and
everything feels so
free i am

free

heart so light and soul so

clean

despite some waging greyish
waves
that i'm just painting
pink

to match the sky and how i feel

they said, you'll be someone else and just the same. they were right.

a written polaroid about being twenty-one

when was the last time i
cried
because being

alive
is the
greatest gift i ever

faced?

the sky in its lover

era

folklore quietly playing

and my eyes watering up
staring

a b o v e

alcohol free fancy drink and
snacks that fill body and my

soul

lesbian romance in the
book on my

legs

and on my mind
wishing hoping

longing

they said, you'll be someone else and just the same. they were right.

a written polaroid about being twenty-one

simplicity that brings me
t e a r s

healing parts i never felt
i'm so soft and light and grateful

and on one of the longest

days

of twenty-twenty-three

i knew

i'll repeat it all tomorrow

they said, you'll be someone else and just the same. they were right.

a written polaroid about being twenty-one

long skirts
my legs feeling the
wind

my hair not listening

and the heat is not too
much

because when something is too
much
i always handle it with

grace

like i always do

they said, you'll be someone else and just the same. they were right.

a written polaroid about being twenty-one

maybe the quiet moments
are so
appreciated now because

all i was, was

loud

and now i learned to
breathe

and also, finally listen

they said, you'll be someone else and just the same. they were right.

a written polaroid about being twenty-one

headfirst, fearless
a lyric so simple

yes, i appreciate the complicated words
like everything i ever went

through but

my heart wants
peace

and to be

fearless

-thank you for teaching me, taylor

they said, you'll be someone else and just the same. they were right.

a written polaroid about being twenty-one

i touched him
directly
where we innocently
feel in
love

as a form of
revenge

two years later,
it disgusts me.

he did not want my
body

but all you craved was
mine.

where's the
connection?

please be hungry for my body
just the way you take my
soul

two aches
in one
can we be
one?

would you..

let me?

they said, you'll be someone else and just the same. they were right.

a written polaroid about being twenty-one

but if the story is over, why am i still writing pages?

taylor swift

death by a thousand cuts

they said, you'll be someone else and just the same. they were right.

a written polaroid about being twenty-one

years ago
i dedicated
lover

by taylor swift

to you

the biggest harry stan i
know

i didn't know they were dating
years ago
not then

i'm a swiftie now
and you probably still love
harry

they fell

apart
just like we did

i don't know if i would stand up
when nobody applauds for
you

we were broken people that made each other

worse.

because sometimes
when you're 17
you don't know

better.

they said, you'll be someone else and just the same. they were right.

a written polaroid about being twenty-one

i wish i could listen to
harry
again
after all this time

i'm still recovering after
two and a half years

yesterday, i finally listened to
lover

again

and i wonder what
could've been
would've been
should've been

you

but we're never getting back
together because you
hate me

and i understand

all that's left is my first ever
tattoo

and me begging you to get
better

it's time to be
fearless again

i say

they said, you'll be someone else and just the same. they were right.

a written polaroid about being twenty-one

i wonder if you know that
we could have been

golden

like both our favorite artists
said

our favorite artists fell apart
like
we
did

and it hurts that
you will never know

that you should have thought of

me

when listening to taylor
maybe

i wish i didn't remember it

all too well because
i surely don't want
to

but my sparkles are back
and i'll be shining
over your sad empty town

they said, you'll be someone else and just the same. they were right.

a written polaroid about being twenty-one

but

never forget the

beautiful tragic love

we had

-060116

they said, you'll be someone else and just the same. they were right.

a written polaroid about being twenty-one

january, 2021
you left me a day before
we would have had
our

meetiversary

the fifth one.
the one i still have tattooed on my
right arm.

it was my first tattoo,
ever.

"ideservebetter2021"
that's what happened when i
changed my laptop password
to when i could not take it

being the day, we decided

to officially be in

love.

and now it's 2023
and i still have that password in and
all i am thinking now is

i deserved better

in 2021,

too.

they said, you'll be someone else and just the same. they were right.

a written polaroid about being twenty-one

what if i said that
even after two and a half
years

i still cannot listen to
certain songs and
i get mad over things you once

said

and i wonder
really deeply wonder if
i impact your life like

that too,

still

-i just know that you don't want to be associated with me
anymore, at all

they said, you'll be someone else and just the same. they were right.

a written polaroid about being twenty-one

you taught me

s i l e n t   c r i e s

which i never could
do and sometimes they are
practical

but i wish
i never needed them
or at least
never would have

l e a r n e d
them
that way

-06012016

they said, you'll be someone else and just the same. they were right.

a written polaroid about being twenty-one

it's been more than three years
since we last spoke
yet i search for you
on every street

every day of my
life

in any man that looks as
old and similar as you might
look like if you actually started
transitioning

in every woman that slightly looks like
the girl i met back then
or the woman i fell in love
with

over all these years
slightly and desperately
craving and aching
breaking and

i sing the one direction
songs at parties
because i know them because of us

i'm just here for taylor

i wonder if you like a song of
hers

I don't wanna live forever, maybe?

those nights are the best ones but the ones with you they

they said, you'll be someone else and just the same. they were right.

a written polaroid about being twenty-one

weren't the best nights
the ones with the most
feeling

and tears and hopelessness and depression and suffering
and

i can listen to the same songs
again
but my therapist said
i'm traumatized

butterflies that turned into

dark clouds forever

and yet i always ached to find the light

again for a

second

i still do this in friendships, too

you were a good friend
an average
lover

the worst thing that could happen to

me

they said, you'll be someone else and just the same. they were right.

a written polaroid about being twenty-one

and yet the closest i ever got to loving
someone

and yet i look for you

on every street

in every woman with brown curly hair and every man
in flannels and soft
features

-i never want to fall in love again (i don't think it
happened after you.)

they said, you'll be someone else and just the same. they were right.

a written polaroid about being twenty-one

there's something about
healing
from your first big love
even after
ages

i still don't listen to
most of
our songs but

i turned on the fairy
lights again

without picturing your touch
that's long lost and
forgotten

they said, you'll be someone else and just the same. they were right.

a written polaroid about being twenty-one

i hosted parties and starved my body
like i'd be saved by a perfect kiss

taylor swift

you're on your own, kid

they said, you'll be someone else and just the same. they were right.

a written polaroid about being twenty-one

i remember being in
high school
in my volleyball
class

wore the shirt i slept
in this
night and
i put a knot in it so it showed my

belly

but i put it down again because
i thought the skinny
girls would think it was
disgusting

i was skinny myself

i was really skinny most of
my life but
most girls were
even skinnier

now i wear a mini
skirt that makes my
bigger belly visible and
yet

i will carry it outside and let it
b r e a t h e

even at my parents'

house

they said, you'll be someone else and just the same. they were right.

a written polaroid about being twenty-one

i worry too much about my
body

sometimes but
the thoughts and fears that i
felt

when i was skinny lost in
diet culture
were so much
worse

skinny people worry about
six pounds
while it's like
nothing for me at this
point

reclaiming my body and gaining this

weight

saved both my body and my

mind

they said, you'll be someone else and just the same. they were right.

a written polaroid about being twenty-one

buying chips
after pole because
the skinny girls who
dance with me
did

i am alone right now but
i buy them
eat them on the
train

and think about how i
wish we could be

friends

the language issues are one
thing that's
manageable
but i crave friends my

age

three years
younger and five
older might be fine

they've been like thirty-something

but they taught me

lots

they said, you'll be someone else and just the same. they were right.

a written polaroid about being twenty-one

being almost double
of my moms' dream
weight for

me
does not make me
half

as lovable

they said, you'll be someone else and just the same. they were right.

a written polaroid about being twenty-one

eating without
starving and
shaking

mostly feels like a
waste

of money and
calories

and i thought i would not
care

until i tried to change my
ways

-the aftermath of an almond mom

they said, you'll be someone else and just the same. they were right.

a written polaroid about being twenty-one

"you can eat as much as you want"

and the tears just
want to drown the whole
apartment but i

swallow food swallow

tears.

"and it's better you eat slowly instead of eating nothing"

look what you
made
me.

"you don't have to worry" (honest)

-was this too much, mom?

they said, you'll be someone else and just the same. they were right.

a written polaroid about being twenty-one

you got to know your
hunger cues are
so destroyed
that you go to eat somewhere

without that pain in your stomach like

why should i eat that
now

when all you did was
eat enough for
once

they said, you'll be someone else and just the same. they were right.

a written polaroid about being twenty-one

not eating because
life feels
hard or because
money is to
worry about is

both

a disaster i don't want to
s t a y

in

they said, you'll be someone else and just the same. they were right.

a written polaroid about being twenty-one

today i was looking at my big
belly that i
wished
for

        and said
      "i want to be your
        friend"

they said, you'll be someone else and just the same. they were right.

a written polaroid about being twenty-one

anytime i
question my own
self

and worry about my
body

i start singing
because my voice

the thing i hated the
most

as a kid

is what reminds me how much worth i

hold

they said, you'll be someone else and just the same. they were right.

a written polaroid about being twenty-one

i have longed for a
bigger body
all my life

because everyone wanted me to be
small

as small as possible

and now i have it and
feel the urge to
hide

subconsciously

but the emotional drainage
fades away

and though i feel my
weight i feel

ten time lighter
because they don't tell you

that at

your *heaviest*

you too can be

your *happiest*

they said, you'll be someone else and just the same. they were right.

a written polaroid about being twenty-one

live my life scared to death,
he'll decide to leave instead

taylor swift

forever winter

they said, you'll be someone else and just the same. they were right.

a written polaroid about being twenty-one

there are colorful
balloons

up in the sky and
the foggiest trees i've ever seen and

you know
you really know it when

the cold air does feel like
evermore and fog is screaming folklore and

she's my forever winter but

i did not want to take never grow up so seriously like

she did maybe i know

colorful balloons hugged by
greyish fog

i was fourteen and you were
seventeen

and your radiance will

stay

-30112016

they said, you'll be someone else and just the same. they were right.

a written polaroid about being twenty-one

they said, you'll be someone else and just the same. they were right.

a written polaroid about being twenty-one

there is something in
accepting your
fathers'
tears
just like your granddads'

while listening
to their

pain
and it is not your

fault

all they do is
trust

you

-and you have their lives inside, their passion in your
hurt, their tears in all your joy

they said, you'll be someone else and just the same. they were right.

a written polaroid about being twenty-one

i keep saying i miss summer
2018

because it's the first summer of me
trying to recover

but actually

every summer brings back
something that feels
flawless

2018 and the smell of
victoria secret's love addict
we meet the man who is her
boyfriend now
and her first boyfriend and

feeling left behind
growing close before falling
apart

an all-male friend group and beer i never drank and
breaking in a kindergarten at
sixteen

running as fast as we
can

and the sea breeze not hitting as hard while writing
tattoo plans i never
went for

they said, you'll be someone else and just the same. they were right.

a written polaroid about being twenty-one

2019 and falling for
one certain
artist

that my friends did not
like
and my healthiest
relationship

paderborn and austria
naked in the woods and
pokemon

glass straws favorite bubble tea and
friends that held me so close i barely knew how i
lost them
making aerial dreams come

true
before i even tried
pole

in 2020
spending my entire summer with the love of my
life who never was the
one no day without the

pole

and school's done forever

2021

maybe that's nothing i'd go back to

but

they said, you'll be someone else and just the same. they were right.

a written polaroid about being twenty-one

2022
firstly taking matters into my own
hands and seeing things
no one else can
share

because they were not theirs to
keep nor lose
my favorite city and a mountain view

i will think of in my eighties
and the trio

everything falling into
place without me ever
believing and the
glowing sea and
gay parties

unexpected made outs and
they're drunk on tequila
i'm drunk on
emotions

feeling love i never felt right before i fell in

love in

2023?

summer love that never was
heavy or even real but
enough to make me
cry and finally feeling like

they said, you'll be someone else and just the same. they were right.

a written polaroid about being twenty-one

myself and
the swifties.

me and healing.

i will only ever find a word
when it's
christmas

and i'm

reminiscing
summer after summer

everything i'll ever ache for

they said, you'll be someone else and just the same. they were right.

a written polaroid about being twenty-one

"and every time i look at you, it's like the first time"

does this count for
l i s t e n i n g
as well? because
every time i hear the
first
guitar notes and

the song and the
chorus and the
goddamn hook i just

it's like i am falling in

love all over and over and over and over and over and
over

again

-fearless

they said, you'll be someone else and just the same. they were right.

a written polaroid about being twenty-one

bad bad things you barely tell
anyone

but someone's to trust and
i told her she's deep in my
heart and she responded with

saying that it's so warm in

there

this is a friendship you
barely

find

once in a lifetime

they said, you'll be someone else and just the same. they were right.

a written polaroid about being twenty-one

whenever i cannot relate to a
song but love it still and
then show it to my
best friend who is
living through the

described world i

i just cry, suddenly

her feelings are mine my feelings are

hers

they said, you'll be someone else and just the same. they were right.

a written polaroid about being twenty-one

you don't know what it's
like
how would you
know?

when you're feeling so deeply that
tears ricochet when you're
proud of
someone
you barely

know

working with children who
struggle at
school and suddenly understand
something
and teenagers who
lost themselves and bring
trouble

but you see their sad faces light
up because of someone
or a passion and

you see another part of

them hidden behind all these
walls and

elderly people who talk about their
past and all just makes me
push myself away with a

they said, you'll be someone else and just the same. they were right.

a written polaroid about being twenty-one

stupid

smile and pretending to rub my
eyes because

i feel all of their
happiness i feel their
sadness i feel

everything at

once

they said, you'll be someone else and just the same. they were right.

a written polaroid about being twenty-one

it's hard to
realize

it's never
over

you just have to know how
to deal with
it

and how much distance
that also
means

-are you healed or are you isolated well enough?

they said, you'll be someone else and just the same. they were right.

a written polaroid about being twenty-one

they say you're losing the
real you but
isn't this what always
happens

when people fall in
love?

melting into their
partners being
close and
connected

i always hated to see it but

now i understand why
holding back and
losing yourself in

love

is an actual

thing

and yet my mind stays conflicted

they said, you'll be someone else and just the same. they were right.

a written polaroid about being twenty-one

they say you're acting

and

and

and everything that's making you
feel free and
connected is

like sand slipping through your

fingers

they said, you'll be someone else and just the same. they were right.

a written polaroid about being twenty-one

laughing
so hard that it never fucking
stops because
your own experiences so
teenage like
it's so

beautiful

healing and realizing
you could have this all
along but

you have your whole
life
left to live

but you holding me and just
being with
me

calmed my soul so
good i'll breathe and
go back to this

time

in every single

bad night

-your warmth is like home

they said, you'll be someone else and just the same. they were right.

a written polaroid about being twenty-one

you'll find your
way you're only
twenty-one

my mom said

and that she tells me about a
lesbian couple at her
gym and how they
had a child and

that it also fine if i don't have

any

because i should be my
first priority and

i should be
happy

it seems like everyday
words but

twelve-year-old me
never would have
believed any of

this

they said, you'll be someone else and just the same. they were right.

a written polaroid about being twenty-one

i'm not even aromantic but

couples just make me
uncomfortable
sometimes

somehow i love to see
lesbians being in love because

i crave that for

myself

but

women and men together?

i cannot picture this
life for
myself

and i don't ever want
to

they said, you'll be someone else and just the same. they were right.

a written polaroid about being twenty-one

where you used to
live there is a parking lot
now and

i remember driving to your
house with my dad when i was
hospitalized

to send you a letter because of the first time you
cut me off

and now it's gone and no one will ever remember
what used to be
there just like the

people

who knew what was going on between
2015 and
twenty-twenty-one

all of that is
buried and

dozens of poems and scars and years

wasted on

you

-nothing ever felt like you did

they said, you'll be someone else and just the same. they were right.

a written polaroid about being twenty-one

one day you're 13 in an emergency room
but one day you're 18 sleeping in your own apartment for
the first
time

one day you're 14 burying the girl you were desperately
in love
with but
one day you're 19 and you're dancing
in front of people for the first
time that love

you and make you feel
seen

one day you're 15 and crying over the way people
call you but
one day you're 20 and not even your
friends remember your old
name anymore

and one day you're 16 and the summer brings a spark of
hope that you still dream of at

21 when you're
in love with every season and
an artist who owns your
heart and the best
friends you ever had

and suddenly i believed taylor was right once

again because this pain wouldn't be for

evermore

they said, you'll be someone else and just the same. they were right.

a written polaroid about being twenty-one

both the polish
language and my
hometown hurt me so
deeply

but aren't they all i
carry in my
sense of
belonging this part of

me i'd never

trade for

anything?

-they both came back to me

they said, you'll be someone else and just the same. they were right.

a written polaroid about being twenty-one

clear blue
water and the sky is
blue with some sparks of
white and there are
trees

and children's laughter and my
ears
drown in the water of
my hometown

and she said all she craves was

autumn but all i say is
look how beautiful the sky
is and now we can enjoy

summer before we enjoy

autumn and we enjoy

winter and then we enjoy

spring

and it makes me realize

how life is never meant to be a
punishment

they said, you'll be someone else and just the same. they were right.

a written polaroid about being twenty-one

headfirst, fearless

-enough said

they said, you'll be someone else and just the same. they were right.

a written polaroid about being twenty-one

this goddamn
meadow
right in this goddamn

city

gives me some haunting sense of
belonging and
carrying my hometown

with me

but without the heavy hurt of
fields and grass and dirty
soil

-i could lay and stay forever

a written polaroid about being twenty-one

and even though everything is so
f i n e
and normal and

life feels
great doesn't

it?

sometimes there's a new
lana song and

a never-ending ache for melancholia

that i can turn on and off

every time i

want it to

it does not get me

stuck

-i even crave some rain and dark leaves

they said, you'll be someone else and just the same. they were right.

a written polaroid about being twenty-one

the people that bullied
you grow up just like
you do

but if you haven't seen them in
eight years

they will stay teenagers and children for
life

and you'll still flinch at
13-year-olds

who'll never be who hurt you but

you're afraid they might

they said, you'll be someone else and just the same. they were right.

a written polaroid about being twenty-one

when i was 14 i realized that
those will be the days
i will talk about

in my 20s

and i have not ever lived the same
again

they said, you'll be someone else and just the same. they were right.

a written polaroid about being twenty-one

my teenage years were
gut-crushing but
sometimes
sometimes i wish i could go

back

-the air felt different

they said, you'll be someone else and just the same. they were right.

a written polaroid about being twenty-one

sometimes i miss
being 15 and high in
love with random
people and
crushes that

crushed
me
that i never even dated
this boy from a few
grades

above

heaven in hiding
the halsey
song

and it was autumn and my best
friend and me
jogging into sunrise and

me running in the rainy

weather

i wasn't miserable was i?

i was miserable,

wasn't i?

was i?

oh what was i?..

they said, you'll be someone else and just the same. they were right.

a written polaroid about being twenty-one

and as i am listening to
a song by an artist you
like
i wonder

how many times i will
make playlists
for girls
who will never get to

see them

they said, you'll be someone else and just the same. they were right.

a written polaroid about being twenty-one

i do not own this
name
anymore
but whenever people talk
kindly

about someone who
has
it

feels like
my broken inner child
gets a pat on

her back

they said, you'll be someone else and just the same. they were right.

a written polaroid about being twenty-one

looking at younger selves is always
like
look how far you've
come

i cannot describe what it
does to me to look at
my aunties' granddaughters and

taylor's younger self and

all of that
darling

growing up does not hurt
but looking back

gives off emotions

i can't explain

they said, you'll be someone else and just the same. they were right.

a written polaroid about being twenty-one

why am i crying,
darling

maybe because younger you
who never saw sense in
relaxing and just watching
a series or a movie
without initiating
damage

who always hated about other people's
music taste
and disregarded anything
feminine

and childish
behavior

spends their sunday on a sofa
watching a series
in a taylor swift apartment
begging to go to the
cinema again

after watching barbie

not listening to anyone but

taylor

making friendship bracelets and
meeting so many amazing
girl friends

they said, you'll be someone else and just the same. they were right.

a written polaroid about being twenty-one

who are mostly
younger but bring out
every single spark

i ever had to

feel

it's okay to cry

you're healing, darling

they said, you'll be someone else and just the same. they were right.

a written polaroid about being twenty-one

this year is going so
fast can someone
please press

pause

they said, you'll be someone else and just the same. they were right.

a written polaroid about being twenty-one

i stopped defining
myself

over words on my therapist's papers
my life turned around

and i've never been

happier

they said, you'll be someone else and just the same. they were right.

a written polaroid about being twenty-one

long, dark hair and a bit of blonde in it and
anime short, light brown hair like a deer and
a smell that haunts
one for
ages pink cotton candy fluff and bloody
showers but i'd die for your
red hat and wet
hair and three months that turned into
a
forever nevermore
and a what if that tasted like
wodka and
regretting and then a taste of
soy cream pasta with
corn, weed and there's
something in your
bedsheets and my skin

which *never, ever*
leaves and smokey
moments a dream that only
made me weak and restless and same mistake

second time same hope and
dreams but never again i
know i know i
know better you
sting and there was more smoke
before and regrets but
i felt so much i am
drowning i am just

they said, you'll be someone else and just the same. they were right.

a written polaroid about being twenty-one

i just want to drown
again

drown me

i want to drown again drown
me

in a way i will never forget but
please be more than just another
part of a poem

that counts the highest
clouds i've ever

reached

-ten years, eight people

they said, you'll be someone else and just the same. they were right.

a written polaroid about being twenty-one

if i ever loved you,
you'll stay a part of
me

whether you want it or
not
a bone-crushing romance or a long lost
friendship you

made me
feeling that strong for people

makes me

me.

i don't care if we hate each

other but if i hate you

i just despise parts of

myself

they said, you'll be someone else and just the same. they were right.

a written polaroid about being twenty-one

you couldn't take
touch

and i couldn't take being
away from

you

-eleven-year-olds don't understand this kind of **violence**

they said, you'll be someone else and just the same. they were right.

a written polaroid about being twenty-one

and they
say that they'd
fall for a girl from time to

time or maybe just
know but it will never
be an option

or anything that ever

matters

it's a
pattern

and a pattern that hurts my

soul

**there's nothing wrong with
you**

-reaching for you from a distance

they said, you'll be someone else and just the same. they were right.

a written polaroid about being twenty-one

we had a
phone call and

it felt like talking to
my grandpa and

you sound like him and
i don't want that

and it's the last thing you want
you're growing older and
i don't want to picture that but

don't you ever leave

-dad

they said, you'll be someone else and just the same. they were right.

a written polaroid about being twenty-one

everyone is falling in
love and i'm falling

behind

-a quote that could not have described it any better

they said, you'll be someone else and just the same. they were right.

a written polaroid about being twenty-one

i don't know how that
happened but
i used to be obsessed with

crime

mainly, because i needed something
worse than my experiences or
thoughts

i think.

the most disgusting hurtful
actions and killing and blood and intense descriptions
and

now i just cry by the
thought of

it

i want to read and watch but i just
can't

reality deeper and i got to admit

'i'm just too soft for all of it'

they said, you'll be someone else and just the same. they were right.

a written polaroid about being twenty-one

reputation by taylor
swift came out
one year before my
name change and

she just gave me an
anthem that i would have
needed back then when i
did not want to
listen to

her.

when i still had to correct everyone at
school on a daily basis and couldn't and as the teachers
forgot after the

holiday and

they said, you'll be someone else and just the same. they were right.

a written polaroid about being twenty-one

they called it out.

they said, you'll be someone else and just the same. they were right.

a written polaroid about being twenty-one

and i just
just could not look up and

answer feeling
like
i
just
got
harassed

in front of

everyone

-the old me could in fact not come to the phone right now
because she's dead

and dead people don't answer.

they said, you'll be someone else and just the same. they were right.

a written polaroid about being twenty-one

i don't recognize me
sometimes

sometimes i wonder
if my chosen name really fits my
face and then someone makes me
a compliment about my

names and if i am

english and then i just say

thank you :)

maybe i do not see
it sometimes because
diana's full of love and
confidence

while m. just
just got lost and drowned
when i see her

i see my hidden self-loathing

but i want her to know
from far away

she's loved

i had to kill her to
save myself but

she's cheering for
me.
i just know.

they said, you'll be someone else and just the same. they were right.

a written polaroid about being twenty-one

when i want to
ask for lesbian romance
novels in the

bookstore

i still do think
twice

and sometimes, i don't.

-don't tell me homophobia is dead

they said, you'll be someone else and just the same. they were right.

a written polaroid about being twenty-one

i want a
wife.

i want my family to
know more than they
do now.

i don't want to bring
someone who might also be a
friend because i always bring
friends to

family events, right?

i want
to stand there with her in a
beautiful dress
saying i
do and

i want them all there.

everyone is supposed to
know because i just want to be
proud and to be in
love

and not afraid anymore like
i was when i was
twelve.

-i hope some of my grandparents will still see it

they said, you'll be someone else and just the same. they were right.

a written polaroid about being twenty-one

you're a bombshell and she's liquid she's soft and sweet
and just a piece of
glass sometimes but you
you know these sharp
edges you
just know they can't *hurt*
someone who's as soft as
caramel inside
frozen frane
not cut by
tense knifes no it's just

a single drop of
silence in *golden*
moment blurring out
surroundings because you're
loud but no one's here to

listen not the real
melting parts that
float together into

hers and outside?

this room's black and grey but
no one knows the depths of
fate and all the sudden

trust to

stay as you

turn into a hurricane of liquids thrown together blend
with her forgetting both your names but-

they said, you'll be someone else and just the same. they were right.

a written polaroid about being twenty-one

on the outside there is bright light but
no one knows.

'cause you're a bombshell locked away and only she
knows 'cause she's

Yours.

-i wrote this about my best friend falling in love

they said, you'll be someone else and just the same. they were right.

a written polaroid about being twenty-one

i wonder of this is
worth writing
about but

....

hours pass.
days pass.
weeks pass.

....

(it was not)

-the men

they said, you'll be someone else and just the same. they were right.

a written polaroid about being twenty-one

it's about facing your
triggers

when they appear
realizing you'll be

okay

i promise

-my best friend comforting me after a relapse

they said, you'll be someone else and just the same. they were right.

a written polaroid about being twenty-one

girl,
the soul that you
are

the way it just
drowns out all my
fears

makes me
fearless makes me

cozy makes me

feel like i can be a teenager in a stable surrounding for a
night

i know it's not that stable and i'm not a teenager but

an illusion of an always loving
family

woke so many emotions in me that

i need a second to
breathe

-l, do you even know how much i love you?

they said, you'll be someone else and just the same. they were right.

a written polaroid about being twenty-one

sometimes i wonder if
they see my scars and don't go like

it's so hard i am
sorry

but more like

i had it hard, like you
probably did

but i see you made
it

maybe i can make it
too?

-and now i understand why my ex-girlfriend never
wanted me to feel sorry for her about that.

they said, you'll be someone else and just the same. they were right.

a written polaroid about being twenty-one

and as i am
growing
i understand the
lyrics that never made

sense
to me so much
more

step by step by step it makes more sense and i can feel
my
brain
changing

they said, you'll be someone else and just the same. they were right.

a written polaroid about being twenty-one

poetry for the people who
were rejected all their
lives and now
the right people and
everyone love
them but they only ever see it as a
hoax because

their inner child just wouldn't

listen

they said, you'll be someone else and just the same. they were right.

a written polaroid about being twenty-one

are you
fearless (taylor's version)?
maybe?

because i'd listen to you all
day and i'd never ever get
tired and my face just keeps
lighting
up

-you don't even exist

they said, you'll be someone else and just the same. they were right.

a written polaroid about being twenty-one

i once had a
dream about
my best friends and
me

riding our
bikes on an elementary
school yard and

new years' day by
taylor swift was playing and
it was the last part and we were all singing it and the

camera went up in the
blue sky and

the music got louder and it felt like a
movie scene

forever captured because

now, this song is about
them

and reputation got closer to my
heart but

never as close as they

will

because almost no one ever
could

they said, you'll be someone else and just the same. they were right.

a written polaroid about being twenty-one

i'm trying so hard
everyday

to not fuck things
up you
know

cautious and fearful and
silent and just
trying

and when this is not
enough because

**no one is perfect all the
time**

it feels like castles
crumbling

and they hug me in their
shambles

telling me that's all i'll ever
be

-i usually don't talk about myself anymore

they said, you'll be someone else and just the same. they were right.

a written polaroid about being twenty-one

"i'm fucking things up"
what about i'm
handling things with more
grace
and more stable inner

monologue

than i did the last
years?

-one can never be free from misbehavior, even taylor said
that

they said, you'll be someone else and just the same. they were right.

a written polaroid about being twenty-one

maybe i don't want to
remember
2021 but maybe that's a
lie

i don't wanna remember the
promiscuity that was no
fun i don't wanna

remember the heartbreaks and obsession cycling and the
damn lockdown but
ashnikko and
breckerfeld the best
workplace i ever

had and
the mothica ep and
growing while facing

fears and
i don't know because now i think my life was never
worse but then i thought it was never

better

-thanks for the reference, taylor

they said, you'll be someone else and just the same. they were right.

a written polaroid about being twenty-one

i love my maturing
face and love my
birthdays
but the first time i was
worried about

a g i n g

was when i was twenty-one
looking at my face
worried about how people
say you'll start decaying at

twenty-five

looking at people younger than
me while i remember times of me always being
youngest and
hating this and
hating that and

aging is a gift
that not everyone gets to
experience

but here i am
looking at my mom
worrying at her face in the

mirror and

my aunts who won't let anyone
call them
grandma and

they said, you'll be someone else and just the same. they were right.

a written polaroid about being twenty-one

my cousin in her mid-thirties but to me she's twenty
something but

now I AM TWENTY SOMETHING
and sixteen seems so young and eighteen too and
i see a woman in the
mirror but

when did i stop being a
little girl?

what now?

will it be okay?

i'm way too young for all these
questions

-every woman is.

they said, you'll be someone else and just the same. they were right.

a written polaroid about being twenty-one

maybe i do not hate
working

maybe it's not what
drains me

maybe it's not like i don't
want a
fulltime job or that

i don't feel
capable

maybe i just hate
working

for some jobs i am not
suited for

-i have never felt this way before

they said, you'll be someone else and just the same. they were right.

a written polaroid about being twenty-one

i do think
about work when i
fall
asleep but

you know
it's so much better to
think about the precious
souls

you met and the
kindness
that lives inside the
team

inside of losing it because
you got to do some
calculations

as a cashier

in repetitive manner

they said, you'll be someone else and just the same. they were right.

a written polaroid about being twenty-one

i remember driving to
that one friend of
mine

going to a bakery
you texting
me that i gotta listen to
conan grey
more

it was april

it was still so
new
you were new and the
group was

i was so excited just praying you would
like
me
that they'd like
me

i will drive to their house again,
in two days
i am listening to conan
grey in the
kitchen

where i cooked for you when you stayed

over

they said, you'll be someone else and just the same. they were right.

a written polaroid about being twenty-one

and it's october
i know you like me
and i know they like me
too

and i'm a few bracelets, friendships and memories
richer

-thank you for being you, j

they said, you'll be someone else and just the same. they were right.

a written polaroid about being twenty-one

my first old name is my dad's initial
my second old name is my
mum's

by rejecting it, am i rejecting
them?

sometimes they still make me
feel like
that

but i'm not rejecting
them

i'm just another butterfly
creating a distance
that was needed

-they read my letters to the court

they said, you'll be someone else and just the same. they were right.

a written polaroid about being twenty-one

your mind is blocking
you more
than

your body
does

i let my body be and
suddenly

it all worked out
be kind to your mind

-half of a chair spin

they said, you'll be someone else and just the same. they were right.

a written polaroid about being twenty-one

you cried
seeing me
for the first time and

i suddenly believed

i was worth

something

again

-j

they said, you'll be someone else and just the same. they were right.

a written polaroid about being twenty-one

you're like a
mirror
i look into seeing

myself

please don't get hurt please don't
please don't make my mistakes but you
have to

you're too old for your
age and i know that you know but

your skin is not scarred but your soul looks like
mine and

please never forget

i'll always be your shoulder to
cry on

your last call when something goes
wrong

i look into your eyes and see

myself

a stronger self

and you don't want to be

protected

but you always will be

-2008

they said, you'll be someone else and just the same. they were right.

a written polaroid about being twenty-one

every girl i ever loved
left a scar on
me

no matter how close she's been

to my heart like
ever

it only means
i opened my heart
again

after years

they said, you'll be someone else and just the same. they were right.

a written polaroid about being twenty-one

i thought there was true
love and i left it all
behind

because it was not them but
ever since i read that quote

"fuck soulmates, i'll love you on purpose"

that's what it should be.
and once in my life

i am rational

no one is perfect or
made for me but
one girl will make it work

and i'll love her.

on purpose.

they said, you'll be someone else and just the same. they were right.

a written polaroid about being twenty-one

i have an ache for the
2010s
somehow
people reading at the pool
instead of being on their

phones

everything seemed much more
simplified

and even though i'm such a phone
person i just

want to go back in time and

be an adult in the 10s

and see if everything would be
different

today

they said, you'll be someone else and just the same. they were right.

a written polaroid about being twenty-one

they're all gold rush girlies and i am
not

i'm so good by halsey

you're ghost

i'm what happened at the bridge of
colors and

you're midnight rain
and maybe it's true that
the loving ones are

boring but

i'll keep shining

they said, you'll be someone else and just the same. they were right.

a written polaroid about being twenty-one

would've could've should've
stayed

delusional

-you are not the exception, you will never learn your
lesson, dianne

they said, you'll be someone else and just the same. they were right.

a written polaroid about being twenty-one

there will be days where
the folds in fitted
bedsheets won't
make me
cry anymore and
i can open the window at
night and

the number eight is finally learning to stay
silent

and those days are
now

even though i thought i'd have to cross
the universe

to ever fucking see
them

they said, you'll be someone else and just the same. they were right.

a written polaroid about being twenty-one

i love you

i don't even know who i
directed these words too right

now because it's

2am and i am done and tired but

i love

i love so much

they said, you'll be someone else and just the same. they were right.

a written polaroid about being twenty-one

three people,
three songs

cardigan
gold rush
foolish one

three people, one truth,
three people, two questions

three people
one similarity

that i'll never stop trying and
never will apologize

for my effort

they said, you'll be someone else and just the same. they were right.

a written polaroid about being twenty-one

i don't want to talk bad
about past me but
in 2021

i've been someone

i don't even want to
remember

they said, you'll be someone else and just the same. they were right.

a written polaroid about being twenty-one

sometimes i think that moving away from
wuppertal would hurt
more

than moving away from my
hometown

yes for sure it stored my
childhood and
nostalgia but

this place holds the first
years of

trying to find my
authentic

life

and living it

they said, you'll be someone else and just the same. they were right.

a written polaroid about being twenty-one

i never wanna be too
old for
playgrounds
in the middle of the
night

the dark, music and just
me

and doing some acrobatic shit that
no one can explain but

it helps with
everything

they said, you'll be someone else and just the same. they were right.

a written polaroid about being twenty-one

a girl who identifies with

"but i won't die for love but ever since i met you, you could have my heart and i would break it for you"

and a girl who relates to

"i can't call it love if i show it"

all the duality of
halsey

a tragedy in
three, four, five, seven hundred acts if i don't

stop
attracting the wrong people

i said that years ago

already

they said, you'll be someone else and just the same. they were right.

a written polaroid about being twenty-one

we live in a world full of
style and new york city
girls while all i ever
wanted is to
stay deep into my

fairytale dreams

spinning in a long skirt while
the sun hugs my hair and

all i'll ever be is a
dreamer full of

imperfections

without planning to change

they said, you'll be someone else and just the same. they were right.

a written polaroid about being twenty-one

maybe there's a world
hidden in raw onions and
sweet coffee and
hugging someone from
college you barely

know

because your heart is just
so full

and all you need to do is
share it all

even though so many adults are
way too fucking
calm about the

right things

they said, you'll be someone else and just the same. they were right.

a written polaroid about being twenty-one

i am not shaming myself into
feeling bad about loving too
deep trying too
hard living the way i
live or talking too
much and just

being

because someone
said
you wouldn't want people around
you who judge you for who
you really are
right

right?

right.

being unapologetically
myself

is everything

i'm tired of living in
shame

they said, you'll be someone else and just the same. they were right.

a written polaroid about being twenty-one

a champagne problems
this is me trying the last American
dynasty girlie a you're losing me
girlie i should have
known

better

they said, you'll be someone else and just the same. they were right.

a written polaroid about being twenty-one

we spent every day together
whenever we
could until the very late
night and you
went home at
3am or i

did

now it's another friday that you
have to

cancel

and 30km between
us
instead of

a not even 3-minute-walk

or the 3min bus
drive we had

for three years

friday is our day and
we will always find
each other

because you're the
best thing that has ever been
mine

you know?

they said, you'll be someone else and just the same. they were right.

a written polaroid about being twenty-one

don't become my dorothea
yet
there's still so

much

for us

-childhood best friends forever and always

they said, you'll be someone else and just the same. they were right.

a written polaroid about being twenty-one

and step by step
so many things
that seemed

i m p o s s i b l e

became
overly exhausting
bearable

on the way to
okay one
day

-one step at a time <3

they said, you'll be someone else and just the same. they were right.

a written polaroid about being twenty-one

i hated this so
much
and it was not

g o o d

either way you
know but

staring through the
rooftop
window
lying on the back

watching the clouds

move

on a bright blue
sky

pretending to be in a
rocket

instead of a way too

tiny room for someone who's
not eleven anymore

i miss where the fries once

were at the

swimming

place

they said, you'll be someone else and just the same. they were right.

a written polaroid about being twenty-one

and the place where my
dad and i
used to
lie there

when he was still in his
forties

and i was like seven

and enjoying a cheeseburger for the first
time

when i was fourteen
and the trips with my best friends' mom and
screaming through the street

so she hears me from her
balcony

and sometimes, my little

tiny

childhood room

they said, you'll be someone else and just the same. they were right.

a written polaroid about being twenty-one

i remember being 14'
and truly realizing
t h o s e
will be the memories that i will look at
forever

as a painful capture of
youth

nothing hurt as much as
wanting to grow up but
losing certain stages of
childhood

and the teenage
years
when you were not

ready for

yes, i had sex already but
yes, i am sad that you will not play outside with the
basketball
and in the fields

and when i realized times have
changed
two years
later

yes i am glad you fell in love for
the first time but
i miss our girls' trips

they said, you'll be someone else and just the same. they were right.

a written polaroid about being twenty-one

why does he matter
more
now

i miss our
girlhood

and even though i was way faster in
cliché milestones

you were always the one to
let go of it
faster

and now you're a grown
woman

living with your
mom

and i'm in my colorful
apartment

with a childlike spirit that
never dies

they said, you'll be someone else and just the same. they were right.

a written polaroid about being twenty-one

i want to dye my hair more
natural i want to wear
flower skirts i want to
have starbucks and listen to blank space i want to
wear pastel colors i want
fine line tattoos i want to leave

my old life
behind

and the bittersweet nostalgia

it made me

feel

they said, you'll be someone else and just the same. they were right.

a written polaroid about being twenty-one

listening to taylor
after a few
exhausting hours
is like coming home to

a loved one
who pulls their arms around
you

and your entire nervous systems

regenerates

pure serotonin
and peace of

mind

they said, you'll be someone else and just the same. they were right.

a written polaroid about being twenty-one

let the woman
go before
us

children said
stairs up the waterslide

i went down with my
dad

years and years
ago

while i always aimed to
be
an adult

now i also seem like
one
and i am

wanting to tell people i am
eighteen but

eighteen is so far
away

already?
the new perspective

scary and sacred

you grow into

it

they said, you'll be someone else and just the same. they were right.

a written polaroid about being twenty-one

step by step

but it takes time to

realize

-twenty-one

they said, you'll be someone else and just the same. they were right.

a written polaroid about being twenty-one

five years ago i wrote
how much this town
hurts
my feelings

three years ago, i still

felt

it

today, all i want to do is
spend time right

there

i may not call it my
home

but a beloved hometown
for sure

-healing means going back too

they said, you'll be someone else and just the same. they were right.

a written polaroid about being twenty-one

it's been so long since i
walked up this
water slide
35kg lighter
with a whole bag of mental

baggage

but suddenly this town
this waterslide
and the look from
above

feels like all the heavy load
of sickness

never ever existed
and suddenly i am
seven
remembering the moments

that were fine
the stairs up were still
slippery
and orange
like my childhood room

and all the food things

changed

nostalgia is
bittersweet but

they said, you'll be someone else and just the same. they were right.

a written polaroid about being twenty-one

i am a grown-up child

again

but this time
for real

they said, you'll be someone else and just the same. they were right.

a written polaroid about being twenty-one

you finally found
yourself

people said
and it never felt more

right

in my
long skirts
hopeless romantic
lesbian thoughts

believing in the good
while changing heavy
eyeliner

to hundred shades of
lipstick

playing taylor all the time
while looking at the halestorm tat

-i had no idea this was the real me

they said, you'll be someone else and just the same. they were right.

a written polaroid about being twenty-one

isn't it
funny how
i wrote a book about
finding myself in every kind of
way

only to realize

not a single thing was
right?

-after apocalypse

they said, you'll be someone else and just the same. they were right.

a written polaroid about being twenty-one

i looked around in a blood-soaked gown
and i saw something they can't take away

taylor swift

you're on your own, kid

they said, you'll be someone else and just the same. they were right.

a written polaroid about being twenty-one

sometimes,
nowadays
i look at my arms and
legs wishing the
scars were not
there but

i do not remember me
without
them i barely remember my life
before i was entirely
covered

in the blink of an
eye

yes, they're a very
characteristically
feature

about me but
i wonder who else i

                    could
                    have
                    been

they said, you'll be someone else and just the same. they were right.

a written polaroid about being twenty-one

no one ever
reacted bad
to seeing me in
short clothes

(no one that made me think
it matters)

even when i was told
how disturbing i'd seem
to everyone

simply
because i tried to take away

what i was too young to
experience or even

k n o w

they said, you'll be someone else and just the same. they were right.

a written polaroid about being twenty-one

i barely can
believe
what i did in my

youngest years

it felt like failure to not be
able to
do this anymore but

there's nothing romantic about
gaps in skin and bloody
bathrooms and trusting
strange men with your
body in an apartment that's
more like your own
soul and

i know. i just know.

they said, you'll be someone else and just the same. they were right.

a written polaroid about being twenty-one

i recognize those
streets
when
i was torn in pieces

and all i wanted was
money

and being desired and i
really thought it was
fun

at least just in my

head
(imagine a sighing scream)

i knew i was a lesbian even before i felt so
many men on my
body

not even in an owning
way just in a
using way

it was(n't) what i wanted.
*(imagine tears on my cold face. it's foggy and you can
barely even see them.)*

on this street
it was ice cold and

one could see
snow
(i love snow!)

they said, you'll be someone else and just the same. they were right.

a written polaroid about being twenty-one

and i tried to
touch him but i
couldn't in his

car

the ten-year-age gap

he carried
my half naked body into his trunk and
he asked me if he could take
pictures and

i let him.

pictures of parts
i just wanted to feel
desired and
loved. *(exclamation mark. screams. banging against a
non-existent wall sobbing, wanting to save younger me)*

he faked tiredness and then anger

and gave me less because i
could not fake

excitement

-fifty

they said, you'll be someone else and just the same. they were right.

a written polaroid about being twenty-one

there was a moment
i looked at my
scars

and never wanted to add
any more of
them

and just wanted them to
leave

-june 2023

they said, you'll be someone else and just the same. they were right.

a written polaroid about being twenty-one

they said, you'll be someone else and just the same. they were right.

a written polaroid about being twenty-one

you're both
out in some other
city

and you're meeting her
boyfriend before he even
knows that i
exist

and i'm over here writing and
eating pasta

not a single bad thought in my
head

just comfortable
silence

they said, you'll be someone else and just the same. they were right.

a written polaroid about being twenty-one

fearless reminds me of
sunshine, being naive
optimistic and
hopeful

a spirit not ruined by the

cruelty of the world
yet

the sound of the song is what i always feel
like

every day is a gift and i just want to
jump
and dance and spin in
circles

and it's easy.
everything just feels so
light.

my mom just called
me saying that she watches all my
pictures saying

i have my glow back

the one i had, when i was only five years old

when the cruelty of the world did not get to me, yet

that i truly seem like myself again after all these years

they said, you'll be someone else and just the same. they were right.

a written polaroid about being twenty-one

maybe this is why it is
my favorite
album

and my favorite
song

because i'm glowing just as

much

-you met me at the right time

they said, you'll be someone else and just the same. they were right.

a written polaroid about being twenty-one

i was listening to
lover again
and for the first
time in ages
i did not think of

him

i thought of you

-midnights girl

they said, you'll be someone else and just the same. they were right.

a written polaroid about being twenty-one

we haven't said
"i love you"
yet

yet we show it
all the time

and i **think** it

all the time

-i'm finally taking my time

they said, you'll be someone else and just the same. they were right.

a written polaroid about being twenty-one

there was a desire
i could barely
explain

something inside our
eyes locking and my heart
racing and knowing i have to
do this in that sudden

moment

you made my body feel
things i thought i had

forgotten

-definitely never been bisexual

they said, you'll be someone else and just the same. they were right.

a written polaroid about being twenty-one

it's not an unhealthy
rush
or maybe not
yet

but i keep reading sapphic
poetry and the tears just

flow

because my friends heard me
crying about just wanting to be
loved since last
winter and

it feels different now, as i'm
healing

calm and passionate and yet i
just can see you from right here right to

twenty thirty something

they said, you'll be someone else and just the same. they were right.

a written polaroid about being twenty-one

i have hurtful memories with
we fell in love in october by
girl in red but

it's october
and like five hours ago we locked
lips for the first time and maybe

maybe i will actually live through this and

fall in love in

october

and we'll be alright

they said, you'll be someone else and just the same. they were right.

a written polaroid about being twenty-one

i thought our first kiss would be
gentle
shy and innocent

but it was more like

fire on fire

soul ties bonding

kiss me like it's the last thing that can stop this world
from

vanishing

yes, gentleness is
great but
it's like we were just
waiting

to let go and get lost in a
moment that i cannot forget or
remember

because i got lost in you
like that was the last thing
that would stop the world from

vanishing

they said, you'll be someone else and just the same. they were right.

a written polaroid about being twenty-one

and maybe
maybe i'm still scared of

love

scared of falling

all those voices in my head
that want to ruin everything but

i got to take my time and

feel?

there's no hurry

isn't it?

and the past is the past

and you're so

precious

that songs make me cry because i just
cannot understand this is

real

they said, you'll be someone else and just the same. they were right.

a written polaroid about being twenty-one

he was sunshine i was midnight
rain taylor
said

but what if you're just
midnights and i'm
sunshine and there's no
rain just stars and no

"him" just

her and her

united in midnight
skies
put together through

sunshine

and if the rain ever starts

pouring it's not
us like, ever

they said, you'll be someone else and just the same. they were right.

a written polaroid about being twenty-one

i don't believe in
coincidences
and i do believe in some

higher energy,
always.

i wanted to make myself a
sunshine bracelet
for myself after i made the

midnight rain one for the soul
that makes brown curls seem like

scary things are not actually
real

i never finished it, it sits here
waiting

unfinished barely started.

and.

and she made me a
sunshine girl
bracelet when i already forgot

about the one i wanted to make
myself.

it should have been this
way.

they said, you'll be someone else and just the same. they were right.

a written polaroid about being twenty-one

there are no coincidences
someone, something's in control of us

and this makes me
believe always,

step by
step

it's the little things but
it's like the opposite of a
paper cut

but the same amount gives us the same

results

-midnight rain & midnights girl

they said, you'll be someone else and just the same. they were right.

a written polaroid about being twenty-one

there's something unusual about being
safe.

about being chosen, on purpose, daily.

there's something in happy tears and i-cannot-believe-
any-of-this tears and listening-to-taylor-and-relating-now
tears.

you're golden and screaming colors and something i
cannot explain because

there's something in knowing everyone else just did not
know how to make me feel

chosen

but you do it like it's
breathing.

they said, you'll be someone else and just the same. they were right.

a written polaroid about being twenty-one

we were not
'soulmates'.
we were a toxic bonding, incompatible to the
core

that could not let go off
each other
regardless of the

suffering.

-nothing left to romanticize about 060116

they said, you'll be someone else and just the same. they were right.

a written polaroid about being twenty-one

taylor hiding her
smile on the original cover of
1989

and me thinking that i'm not good enough
to be appreciated and
loved in a romantic

way

turning into

1989 (taylor's version)
being the first cover taylor ever
s m i l e d

on and

me meeting the girl who shows me

all of my wildest dreams and ways i need to be fully
loved

are not impossible

i just never found anyone who
got it 100 percent

right

they said, you'll be someone else and just the same. they were right.

a written polaroid about being twenty-one

she danced with me to
lover

she made me a paper ring with
fearless written on
it on her
knees asking me to see the eras

movie

she wiped my tears when i was
shaking when fearless started
at the movies

she made me a chocolate
box with taylor quotes and
wrote me a poem
with more

of her references

i was singing betty lyrics into

her face and had to look

away.

-no one else could do that, ever ever ever

they said, you'll be someone else and just the same. they were right.

a written polaroid about being twenty-one

after being too much of everything

but if I'm all dressed up

there's no feeling like being desired for both authenticity

they might as well be lookin' at us

and my body after i was told my desires don't make sense

and if they call me a slut

for years but she touches me like

you know it might be worth it for once

there have been people before but she erased the
marks they left on me
with her soul and bare
hands

they said, you'll be someone else and just the same. they were right.

a written polaroid about being twenty-one

"i understand you being scared. but it's exactly what you need right? you don't have to dive in headfirst again, you can

grow in love instead of *falling* "

-words from berlin, in a cologne train, drained but happy

they said, you'll be someone else and just the same. they were right.

a written polaroid about being twenty-one

i don't owe men
anything

and they should just stay
fucking sane

being a lesbian is
empowering

sometimes

i was not able to tell them
why they should stop
touching me and
why i pushed them

away

but i knew it deep
down

and listening to a new
carlie song on a
comfy night
bus

after my first ever concert
alone

seeing the band that made me *me*
even though my genre
changed makes me feel more
independent than
ever

-growing up can feel so good

they said, you'll be someone else and just the same. they were right.

a written polaroid about being twenty-one

a song from her self-titled
debut
(which reminds me of taylor, all too well)
that i haven't heard
live

since i was fifteen
singing it on stage
in front of 600 people

no stage experience, ever
but ready to be
brave

and now at 21
with a way better voice
and a way better life

screaming it away

for my little me

who'd grow up to be everything she ever wanted to

be

happier.

they said, you'll be someone else and just the same. they were right.

a written polaroid about being twenty-one

late night bus at
midnight
after seeing this band
at 21
that i first saw at 12
now *alone*
now **alive**
now ***as a woman***

made by lzzy hale
when i still was a little girl
hanging by a thread

-where did the time go?

they said, you'll be someone else and just the same. they were right.

a written polaroid about being twenty-one

not afraid to dance it
out
to feel the music
screaming
not caring what anyone
thinks about
me

feeling free
with every fiber of my
body

-healing at halestorm

they said, you'll be someone else and just the same. they were right.

a written polaroid about being twenty-one

a fading 13 on my left
hand
a halestorm tattoo
on my right
wrist

two worlds collide

but they're both me.

-when you're 21, aren't you also 20, 15, 13, 9 as well?
you're everything you ever were

right below the
surface

they said, you'll be someone else and just the same. they were right.

a written polaroid about being twenty-one

"who would you be,
if your anxiety wasn't
right in your
way?"

that's what people asked me
before but
they should see me with
her

because she makes me feel
safer than anything i knew
before

and i can explore who i
am
when nothing's holding me
back

-she makes me *fearless*

they said, you'll be someone else and just the same. they were right.

a written polaroid about being twenty-one

there's no feeling like
seeing your favorite
song
on a big screen
getting up to scream it
holding your hands and
feeling it with
you
doing anything that you have the
time of your
life

-my hands were shaking, but I usually am this way

they said, you'll be someone else and just the same. they were right.

a written polaroid about being twenty-one

thirty something girls around us
twenty-something girls
who all feel the
same

four girls
standing in a circle
arm in arm in
arm

singing long live to each
other
even though the movie is
over

and people are leaving
but we don't
and i won't ever leave
you

hand in hand in
hand
screaming long live
spinning in circles

jumping around and
not caring at all because

taylor said being excited is nothing to be
ashamed
about

-this is our place, we make the rules

they said, you'll be someone else and just the same. they were right.

a written polaroid about being twenty-one

my aching is
incredible

five years ago,
i wrote about fictional
feelings that i never
had

today i just think of your
face and your body and how you make me feel
in every kind of
way

it's far from fictional

you're mine.

i still cannot believe
it.

i ache for the passion we
have that i craved for my
entire life.

i ache for your sweet smile and every second i want to
spend with
you in a world, just
us

and between sweet smiles and burning
heat there's us.

everything i ever wanted.

-maybe my fears will finally die

they said, you'll be someone else and just the same. they were right.

a written polaroid about being twenty-one

you're insane for
feeling everything so
deeply,
they said.

and i just carried on with my
life
thinking no one would ever
understand

not understand, but
relate

and then i met her.
our bodies and minds
intertwining.

and suddenly i knew
this was what i was aching
for

when nobody else understood

-midnights girl

they said, you'll be someone else and just the same. they were right.

a written polaroid about being twenty-one

she feels so
good
my mind is hitting
replay over and
over and
over and
over

and this is only the
beginning

-she drives me crazy without even touching me

they said, you'll be someone else and just the same. they were right.

a written polaroid about being twenty-one

the fact that we
did it to taylor
in the background

and the dark room
lit up my
fears
for a second

and i collapsed next to you while
lover was
playing

without ever even thinking of

what once has been

shows me i am healing

and i'm ready for a life

with her

-god. please touch me again.

they said, you'll be someone else and just the same. they were right.

a written polaroid about being twenty-one

i looked into the
mirror looking just like
travis kelce
with lipstick on my face and
she looked like taylor
with her lipstick slightly messes up but
still there

they're not trying to hide
it

and neither do we

they said, you'll be someone else and just the same. they were right.

a written polaroid about being twenty-one

to picture her wet
warmth and the sounds she
makes and how she
held on to
me

just enough to let me
yearn for her
again

-her beauty is unmatched

they said, you'll be someone else and just the same. they were right.

a written polaroid about being twenty-one

it's not a gold rush
it's more like thinking love is burning red but

now knowing it's
golden.

it's not like a huge forest fire
burn down and extinct

it's like little flowers

growing slowly

and every time we meet and
every time we touch

it just grows bigger and more

steady and i want to keep
showering it in

affection

i'd say this is too good to be
true but it's just what we

deserve

they said, you'll be someone else and just the same. they were right.

a written polaroid about being twenty-one

stop thinking
it will turn out
like all the other
ones

give it a

chance

they said, you'll be someone else and just the same. they were right.

a written polaroid about being twenty-one

it's october 2023
i am on my way to the
main station
from uni and the sun is
shining

my hands freezing for the first time in
forever

listening to maroon
and i remember it
all too well

october 2022

in the morning
in the bus to uni
listening to maroon

realizing

my life would never be the same again

they said, you'll be someone else and just the same. they were right.

a written polaroid about being twenty-one

i only ever knew
obsession

so of course, feeling

calm and safe is

frightful

-turns out i never was in love

they said, you'll be someone else and just the same. they were right.

a written polaroid about being twenty-one

the fact that 2016 is
far away enough that i
forgot a main emotional
event
because i never documented
it enough

and only the pictures and texts to something
i thought was the first time i saw
a certain band

brought back tiny memories

that used to be so

present

but i'm not 14 anymore not even 16 or
18 well not even
20

25 is closer than 16 and I am
growing and escaping i'm so young but

not as young as my mind thinks it

is

-i'll never stop documenting my life

they said, you'll be someone else and just the same. they were right.

a written polaroid about being twenty-one

i'm meant for
one-time things
hard feelings and

regrets

and not feeling a thing
touching people who i
dislike

it's like i get all i ever wanted and lose
it

a second later

because my feelings never
match with anyone

else's

they said, you'll be someone else and just the same. they were right.

a written polaroid about being twenty-one

it's just me and the
snow that just came
falling down
that makes me leave the

house

come clean
and live the way i want

to

-it's a real dreamy december start

they said, you'll be someone else and just the same. they were right.

a written polaroid about being twenty-one

they said, you'll be someone else and just the same. they were right.

thank you for reading. now text me your favorite taylor swift song to @eternallyenchantedx or @swyftiecate :)

i love you so much.

there's nothing else to say, really.

let's see how 22 will be.

until then

fearlessly,

diana